# To Everything
## A Season

# *To Everything A Season*

*Janet Campbell*

Paper Doll

© J. Campbell, 1997

First published in 1997 by
Paper Doll
Hutton Close
South Church
Bishop Auckland
Durham

All rights reserved
Unauthorised duplication
contravenes existing laws

ISBN: 1 86248 006 0

Typeset and Printed by
Lintons Printers, County Durham.

*For*
*Alex and Jean*

# CONTENTS

| | |
|---|---|
| Farewell Winter | 1 |
| Solace | 2 |
| Requiem | 3 |
| The Prodigal | 5 |
| Welcome | 6 |
| The Optimists | 7 |
| The Wind | 9 |
| March | 10 |
| The Frontier Folk | 11 |
| Spring | 11 |
| Charity | 13 |
| Enchantment | 16 |
| The Donkey's Hymn | 18 |
| Easter Hymn | 19 |
| The Oyster Catchers | 21 |
| The Visitor | 22 |
| Easter | 24 |
| May | 25 |
| The Cuckoo | 26 |
| Lament for the Gorse | 27 |
| Later | 28 |
| The Parting of the Ways | 28 |
| Regeneration | 30 |
| Summer | 32 |
| A Moat Removed | 33 |
| The Bees | 35 |
| The Killjoys | 37 |
| Nobody's Child | 38 |
| Beside the Sea | 40 |
| For Whom the Heather Weeps | 42 |

| | |
|---|---:|
| In Memoriam | 44 |
| September | 45 |
| October Tapestry | 46 |
| Autumn | 49 |
| The Harvest | 50 |
| The Little Mother | 52 |
| October | 53 |
| Jolly Good Show | 54 |
| The Last Laugh | 55 |
| Our Robin | 56 |
| Hallowe'en | 57 |
| Guy Fawkes | 59 |
| Lest We Forget | 60 |
| The Wren's Prayer | 61 |
| Hope | 63 |
| December Delighted | 64 |
| Winter Wonders | 65 |
| The Donkey's Carol | 67 |
| Compassion | 69 |
| The Little Beggar-Boy | 72 |

# FAREWELL WINTER

Cold Winter's grip is not so strong.
For Spring to come we won't wait long.
The signs are there now ev'ry day.
Soon Winter will be on her way.
When we arise the day to greet,
no longer do we drag our feet.
The days are longer.  There's more light.
At four o'clock it's still quite bright.
Our feathered friends, they seem to know
that Winter hasn't long to go.
At dawn they congregate to sing.
The lady soon some food will bring.
With patience they await their feed,
some crumbs, some fat, a plate of seed.
And though the north wind, it doth blow,
a sure sign of approaching snow,
in gutters icicles abound
and frost rock hard has made the ground,
take heart because the Winter's old.
Soon she'll let go her feeble hold
and Spring will come.  Just look around
for new life stirs below the ground.
Brave little snowdrops peeping through,
not far behind come crocus too.
As the days are getting longer
so the sun is getting stronger.
Until at last, with all its might
cold, dark Winter it puts to flight.

# SOLACE

They left the Garden, they had loved,
the Paradise they'd shared.
Of finding happiness again
the two of them despaired.

As out into the world they went,
there came a fall of snow.
This was a new experience.
It added to their woe.

As Eve looked at her flowers which
were covered by the snow.
She realised how much they'd lost.
Her tears began to flow.

An angel had compassion and
came down to comfort Eve.
He held her gently by the hand
and told her not to grieve.

He lifted up his hand to pluck
a snowflake from the air.
When he unclasped his hand there was
a flower lying there.

He gave the little flow'r to Eve.
He bade her look around.
And through her tears she saw a mass
of white flow'rs on the ground.

Eve wiped away her tears and smiled
the little flow'rs to see,
and legend has it, that is how
the snowdrop came to be.




# REQUIEM

Each morning I go out with crumbs,
some water and some seed.
In winter when it's cold I like
to give the birds a feed.

As I was coming back to-day,
I looked down at the ground.
Just below the kitchen window
a little corpse I found.

A pair of wings lay on the ground
beside the kitchen door.
To eat my food this little chap
alas would come no more.

He must have hit the window that
same morning in full flight.
I'd had fatalities before.
Most had been killed outright.

That day I had let out the cats
before the birds were fed.
They'd be unable to resist
a chaffinch lying dead.

I gathered up the little wings,
I'll bury him I thought
and in the walled-in garden I
will find a pleasant spot.

Between some clumps of snowdrops and
beneath the holly tree,
I dug a little grave and hoped
content there he would be.

Ah how incongruous life is,
a little chaffinch dead,
and all because that winter I
the little birds had fed.

# **THE PRODIGAL**

It's very cold.  It looks as if
the winter's here to stay.
The ground is white but I don't care
the sun came back to-day.

Our house is built upon a hill,
on a north facing site.
The summer sun shines down all day
from morning until night.

But in December when the sun
sinks lower in the sky,
it disappears behind the hill,
an unseen passer-by.

Because we're not warmed by the sun
it gets extremely cold.
For two months winter is entrenched.
She won't let go her hold.

The ground is hard.  The snow and ice
seem set on a long stay.
If we were only touched by sun
it all would melt away.

"Will winter ever end? " we ask.
Yes there will come a day,
when February's very young
the sun comes back to stay.

It's very cold. It looks as if
the winter's here to stay.
The ground is white, but I don't care,
the sun came back to-day.


## WELCOME

I'm feeling cheerful even though
it's a cold, wintry day.
The sun came back hip, hip hooray.
The sun came back to-day.

I said to him, "I'm glad you're back.
Wherever have you been?"
He winked and said, "Now that I'm back,
your windows need a clean."

# THE OPTIMISTS

With February almost gone
no more could I delay,
so somewhat fearfully I to
the garden made my way.

This year I'd left it to survive
the winter on its own
Now it was time for me to reap
the harvest I had sown.

Some plants would have succumbed, I knew,
because of the hard frost,
but hopefully I'd find that not
too many had been lost.

The shrubs and bushes all looked dead,
it was quite desolate.
A rabbit that I chanced upon
ran out the garden gate.

As I was coming back I saw
some hoof marks on the ground.
Regrettably to my garden
some sheep their way had found.

Both sheep and rabbits had it seemed
dined well at my expense.
Added to that I'd need to pay
someone to mend the fence.

My garden looked so bare and dead
it filled me with despair.
Then something caught my eye and I
of life became aware.

The ground was hard and it still had
a covering of snow,
though there was frost some little flow'rs
were managing to grow.

There were some snowdrops 'neath a bush
in one of the flow'r beds.
Quite unconcerned in the cold wind
they shook their little heads.

They in their innocence dispersed
the cloud above my head,
"Take heart," they whispered on the wind
"Not ev'rything is dead."

I'll mend the fences, fix the gates,
some seed I'll sow and then
in summer will the Phoenix from
the ashes rise again.

# THE WIND

He's restless, energetic and
he likes to cause a stir,
and if he goes a bit too far
our wrath he will incur.


A madcap blower he enjoys
a little bit of fun.
He'll blow our hats off,
then he'll laugh as after them we run.


He likes to waken us at night
rattling the window pane.
He has a fund of tricks with which
he us will entertain.


He blows from north, south, east or west
and it affects his mood.
When he blows in from south or west
his humour will be good.


And when he blows in from the north
a sure sign we'll have snow,
our feet will turn to blocks of ice.
Our noses they will glow.


There's one side of his nature that's
abhorred by man and beast.
He's bitter and resentful when
he blows in from the east.

Sometimes he's hardly there at all,
a soft and gentle breeze.
"I hope you've not forgotten me,"
he murmurs to the trees.


## MARCH

Rampaging like a lion or
as gentle as a lamb,
a blusterer, a braggart or
quite self-possessed and calm.

We never know what to expect,
what like the day will be.
He doesn't even know himself
just which mood we will see.

A baffling paradox for him
'tween Spring and Winter caught.
Should he side with Winter or
with Spring throw in his lot?

Accept him as he is.  I think
that is the best advice.
Ignore his tantrums,
just enjoy a day that he is nice.

## THE FRONTIER FOLK

It's just the tonic that we need
when flow'rs begin to grow
And little shoots appear above
the winter's frost and snow.
The gentle little snowdrops are
the first the earth to grace.
They all that winter has to hurl
will turn and bravely face.
And flanking them a step behind
the crocus can be found.
Their purple, white and yellow hues
a patchwork on the ground.
The last to come are daffodils
they too put on a show,
they cloak the ground in yellow just
as Spring prepares to go.


## SPRING

The winter's old and feeble now
the signs are there each day.
There's promise of good things to come
for Spring is on her way.

The days are getting longer and
it's light until quite late,
and for the sun to warm the earth
we won't have long to wait.

In a short while the birds the call
of nature will obey.
They'll find a mate and build their nests
in which their eggs to lay.

Likewise the creatures of the wild
are looking for a mate.
The female then must find a lair
in which to procreate.

The ground is ploughed.  The farmer wants
a flat, calm day to sow.
In grassy fields the early lambs
are racing to and fro.

The hazel and the willow trees
with catkin flow'rs abound.
The bare trees, now in bud, will soon
with fresh, green leaves be gowned.

Snowdrops in drifts carpet the ground
and there are crocus too,
with daffodils not far behind,
their shoots are peeping through.

Yes, Spring is on her way at last.
Of that there is no doubt
and when she does appear she will
winter completely rout.

# CHARITY

She laid her bundle gently down
beneath a willow tree,
then sat a while and thought about
what her next move should be.

Five times she had gone up the hill,
approached the farm with dread
and warily the yard had crossed
to reach the farmer's shed.

A few days back she had been forced
to shelter in that shed.
Her time was very near. She had
to make herself a bed.

That very night into the world
six kittens made their way.
Surrounded by the straw, draught-proof,
cosy and warm they lay.

Next morning when the mother heard
dogs barking down below
she knew it would be dangerous
and she would have to go.

In terror of all dogs she spent
the day in abject fear,
afraid to leave her kittens lest
a collie would appear.

She waited till the farmer had
the dogs locked up at night
and then she ventured out to hunt
to sate her appetite.

The next day, bright and early
she arose when it was light.
She'd tarried long enough, now she
must orchestrate their flight.

Now there she sat, relieved but tired,
Behind her lay the farm,
in front a stream she'd need to cross,
This filled her with alarm.

It was impossible. She in
the current would be caught.
The more she studied it she thought
it was with danger fraught.

The willow had been watching as
she'd slowly made her way.
Carrying the kittens from the farm
had taken her all day.

The willow found that as she watched
her admiration grew,
and now that cat's predicament
instinctively she knew.

The willow wanted desp'rately
to help the little cat.
A thought occurred to her,
she smiled. Perhaps I could do that.

The willow with great tenderness
upon the water spread
her branches that the little cat
a path could safely tread.

The cat when all were safe, unto
the tree her thanks made known,
"I never can repay you for
the kindness you have shown."

And ever since the willow has
grey, furry flow'rs in Spring,
like the kittens in the legend
they to her branches cling.

# ENCHANTMENT

I stumbled on a secret place
by accident one day,
a place that was enchanting,
it quite took my breath away.
I'd wandered off the beaten track
into a wood had strayed,
the trees were thick and I my way
with difficulty made.
The branches of the silver birch
clawed at me as I went,
on slowing down the trespasser
they seemed to be intent.
But just when I was thinking that
perhaps return I should,
I came upon a clearing in
the middle of the wood.
A wave of colour greeted me,
a vivid sea of blue
for bluebells carpeting the ground
in wild profusion grew.
I stood quite hypnotised and gazed,
I thought, that of this glade,
Impressionists a masterpiece
most surely would have made.
I understood just why the birch
were loath to let me through,
and why they'd fiercely guarded it
and hidden it from view.
It was a place by man untouched

a garden wild I'd found,
I felt a bit like Moses when
he stood on holy ground.
Reluctantly at last I turned
my back upon the glade,
I left the sunlit clearing
and went back into the shade.
The silver birches, as I passed,
more yielding seemed to be.
I think they knew their secret, they
could safely trust with me.

# THE DONKEY'S HYMN

It was the first time he had had
a rider on his back
and now with care he picked his way
along the hillside track.

Some men had untied the young colt
in Bethany that day.
They'd put some garments on his back
and then led him away.

Just outside Bethany they stopped
for waiting in that place
his rider stood, a man with such
compassion in his face.

Around the donkey people strewed
palm branches on the ground
and with cries of Hosanna did
the hills about resound.

It's very strange, the donkey thought,
this man a king must be
and yet He's chosen for his steed
a humble beast like me.

As they approached Jerusalem
nearing their journey's end,
the donkey's thoughts were of that day,
What did it all portend?

That day he often would recall
how fate on him bestowed
that he should be the one a king
would ride along the road.


### EASTER HYMN

He in Gethsemane that night
had spent the time in prayer.
There came a band of soldiers led
by Judas the betray'r.
To trial he was brought.
In Him Pilate no fault could see
but sentenced Him to death for fear
rebellion there would be.

They put a robe on Him, a crown
of thorns upon His head.
Upon His back they put a cross,
along the road Him led.
His strength was almost gone and when
He stumbled and did fall,
a passer-by His cross did bear
out through the city wall.

On Calvary the Son of Man
was on a cross hung high,
on either side of Him two thieves

were also left to die.
Upon the cross above His head
an inscription had been nailed,
in Hebrew, Greek and Latin it
as King of Jews Him hailed.

His mother and His friends were there
standing below the cross
and on the ground some soldiers for
His clothes a dice did toss.
The sun by an eclipse was hid
that at mid-day began.
It moved an officer to say,
"This was a righteous man."

They put His body in a tomb,
a cave dug into rock.
A stone was put outside the cave,
it would the entrance block.
When friends of His went to the tomb
after the Sabbath day,
they found out that just as He'd said,
He'd risen that same day.

# THE OYSTER CATCHERS

I'm sure I heard them calling on
the river bank last night,
that distinctive kleep, kleep, kleeping
pic, pic if they're in flight.
The flocks will soon be breaking up
and in April or May
the males will woo the females with
a loud courtship display.

They in the sand or shingle a
depression will have made,
a scrape that's either lined or bare,
in it the eggs are laid.
The two to four buff coloured eggs
their brood is for the year.
The chicks soon after they are born
can run if danger's near.

From late on in the summer on
the sea shore they will be,
large flocks will comb the beaches for
the harvest from the sea.
For cockles, mussels, limpets and
small crabs and shrimps they seek
Which they can then break open with
their orange chiselled beaks.

They are immaculate and in
their plumage black and white,

with orange beak and long pink legs
a most attractive sight.
On seashore, shingle or inland,
wherever they may be,
the oyster catchers never fail
to charm and int'rest me.


## THE VISITOR

This winter we have company,
a guest has come to stay,
she is not at all demanding,
in fact she sleeps all day.

I met her first some weeks ago
when I made up our bed,
she was lying on the pillow.
I thought that she was dead.

I gently put my finger down
to touch one fragile wing.
Imagine my surprise when to
my finger she did cling.

Her wings she did unfold and when
before me they were spread,
I saw that this small Tortoiseshell
most surely was not dead.

I put her in a room where the
intrusions would be few,
and left in peace, I hoped that she
would sleep the winter through.

I left her on the window ledge
thinking that there she'd stay.
When next I went to look for her
I found she'd flown away.

I searched the room. Eventu'lly
behind the bedroom door
I spotted her with folded wings,
asleep upon the floor.

I go once a day to check
that she's still lying there,
this little butterfly with whom
we lodgings gladly share.

In late Spring I will let her go,
April or May will do.
And then my little butterfly
I'll fondly bid adieu.

## EASTER

Excited little children eating their Easter eggs.
A fluffy yellow chicken with long bright orange legs.
Serried ranks of daffodils parading on the ground.
The little lambs, achasing each other round and round.
Emblem of Christ's suffering, the cross on which He died.
Resurrection the third day. He rose as prophesied.

## EASTER

Easter
Painted eggs
to roll downhill
Primroses and daffodil
Fluffy chickens hatching out
Little lambs, skipping about
Joyful hymns in churches sung
The cross on which
Jesus was hung
Easter.

# MAY

Of all the months, May is the one
that pastures are most green
and grazing them contentedly
the cattle can be seen

The grass is young and vigorous,
it lush and long does get,
a mantle, fresh and green, untouched
by the hot sun as yet.

The trees, no longer bare, are in
their greenest gowns arrayed,
their parasols of leafy growth
provide a fragrant shade.

The nights are tranquil.  It's light late,
there's time to stand and stare
and listen to the sweet bird song
upon the ev'ning air.

# THE CUCKOO

We're glad to hear the first cuckoo,
it means that Spring is past.
We smile and say, "The cuckoo's back
and summer's here at last."

She first appears some time in Spring,
til Autumn she will stay.
You'll most likely hear her calling
towards the end of May.

She's looking for a nest in which
one of her eggs she'll lay
so that her young when it is hatched
will have a place to stay.

The owners of the nest will feed
their uninvited guest,
quite unaware that they have got
a cuckoo in their nest.

The young cuckoo, when it is hatched,
will other young eject
that the parent birds' attention
from him will not deflect.

The cuckoo's call awakens us
as soon as it's daylight,
it can be quite monotonous
from morning until night.

# **LAMENT FOR THE GORSE**

Our house above a valley's perched,
we have a lovely view
and ev'ry season alters it,
there's always something new.

A road dissects the valley and
above it are some hills.
In summer months the gorse down them
exuberantly spills.

In May the flow'rs are at their best,
prolifically they grow.
From hill and hedgerow radiates
an amber, yellow glow.

Alas this year the gorse is dead,
a martyr to the cold.
It, in all of its glory, we
this month will not behold.

For miles around the bushes are
burnt brown, of flow'rs stripped bare.
A few have managed to survive
but sadly they are rare.

My gaze oft lingered on the gorse
and now it is no more,
For its departure from my world
I grieve. My heart is sore.

An ecological mishap,
a species near extinct,
it bodes ill for our planet earth.
The signs are quite distinct.


## LATER.

Perhaps the picture's not as bleak.
I wrote this in despair.
Did I imagine it to-night,
new growth on what was bare?


## THE PARTING OF THE WAYS

It was a lovely night and so
after we had our tea
we hopped into my sister's car
and drove down to the sea.

After a very pleasant run
we homeward made our way,
ambling along, enjoying what
was left of a nice day.

Relaxed and most content were we
till suddenly ahead
upon the road we saw a bird,
a partridge lying dead.

It must have been hit by a car,
it had been killed outright.
Its mate beside it stood perplexed,
a most distressing sight.

To wildlife dead upon the road
we both were well-inured,
The carnage caused by man and car
a fact of life endured.

But oh, how sad it was to see,
the mate's bewilderment.
It of the blow, bestowed by fate
was wholly innocent.

This little Adam now no more
would wander with his Eve
and together through the hayfields
no more a path would weave.

On side roads, if it's clear behind,
would it cost much to brake?
These roads are seldom busy,
there's a little life at stake.

But no. Man has his ego and
he mustn't be thought soft.
Avoid a creature on the road?
Such action would be scoffed.

# REGENERATION

I'd been working in the garden
from early in the day.
That ev'ning after tea to it
again I made my way.

It was a pleasant ev'ning,
a perfect night in June,
no sign was there of midges that
would the perfection ruin.

This time it was for pleasure I
went through the garden gate,
upon the garden seat I planned
to sit and contemplate.

I sat down on the wooden seat,
my gaze fell on the ground,
where some little garden spiders
were scurrying around.

A butterfly came flitting by
but settle she could not.
A big, fat bumble bee among
the flow'rs for pollen sought.

I heard some swallows twittering,
an oyster catcher call,
a blackbird, warbling in the trees
and wrens upon the wall.

Up on the roof the jackdaws seemed
on bickering intent,
and somewhere high up on the hill
a curlew did lament.

The fragrant scent of blossom from
the trees hung in the air
and of the freshly mown grass
I too became aware.

I sat perhaps an hour or more,
with Nature I communed,
to sights and sounds and perfumes were
my senses finely tuned.

The light was failing when at last
I homewards made my way
in tranquil state of mind and with
all cobwebs blown away.

# SUMMER

The summer time is here, The days
are long and hot and bright.
Relentlessly the sun shines down
from morning until night.

The ev'nings are more gentle,
it is cooler but still bright.
It's much more pleasant out at night
than in the harsh sunlight.

The bees are buzzing in the flow'rs,
in sacs they'll pollen stow
and butterflies, haphazardly
are flitting to and fro.

The gardens now with flow'rs in bloom
are looking at their best,
the veg'tables parade in rows
where weeds have been suppressed.

The fruit on tree and bush has formed,
the insects' work is done.
The fruit is left now for a while
to ripen in the sun.

The flymos, mow'rs and strimmers too
are busy night and day,
they, out of hibernation, strive
to keep the grass at bay.

The wild flow'rs in the verges make
a colourful display
and in the fields the grass, knee high
will soon be cut for hay.

With bringing up their young the birds
have little time to spare,
but not too busy for their songs
to fill the ev'ning air.

Yes, summer's here again.  For us
the pace of life is fast.
It's just as well, however nice
that summer doesn't last.


## A MOAT REMOVED

I think that for most of my life
I've looked but have not seen
but now unshuttered eyes observe
an ever-changing scene.

Though always they've been here with us,
always been growing there,
of the wild flow'rs in the hedgerows
I am much more aware.

And now in middle age I make
the time to stand and stare,
and look along the hedgerows for
a garden wild grows there.

I marvel at the harmony
of Nature's colour schemes,
for in her random harvest
there's no colour clash it seems

From April till October
the wild flow'rs are on show
and just as one variety fades
another starts to grow.

This colourful display until
October it will last,
wave after wave of Nature's troops
will vividly sweep past.

Quite early on in May and June
the bluebells are on view
and then the wayside places all
are carpeted in blue.

Next come in drifts, cow parsley mixed
with clumps of poppies red
and here and there White Campion
does delicately tread.

July brings pockets of wild peas
that squat upon the ground
and dwarfing them are Foxgloves in
a pale magenta gowned.

By August spiky thistles bloom,
their flow'rs a purple hue

and Scabious and Harebells blen
in diff'rent shades of blue.

By September and October
fewer flow'rs are to be seen,
and we are coming to the end
of Mother Nature's paean.


## THE BEES

A memory of childhood that
I can recall with ease
is the time I spent each summer
in studying the bees.

Our blue geranium bushes
flow'red early in July
and to this magnet all the bees
from roundabout would fly.

From dawn till dusk the bushes hummed
with many bees at work
and so that I could watch them I
upon the path would lurk.

With his small, fat, furry body
and wings of filigree,
of all the bees, the bumble bee
my fav'rite had to be.

I used to catch them in a jar,
the better them to see.
I'd hold them close to look at them
and then I'd set them free.

I once kept one all night inside
a jar beside my bed,
I went to set him free next day
and found that he was dead.

I never more imprisoned bees,
I wanted them to live,
the ignorance that killed the bee
I found hard to forgive.

These summers spent among the bees
I never once was harmed.
Unlike the wasps, bees only sting
when angry or alarmed.

My flow'r beds, I have filled once more
with blue geranium,
my garden with the sound of bees
in summer's sure to hum.

So honey bee or bumble bee
or little wild, brown bee,
you're very welcome in my flow'rs
for still you pleasure me.

# **THE KILLJOYS**

In summer ev'nings when it's cool,
the sun's glare not so bright,
you'll find me in the garden
as long as there is light.

The early summer ev'nings are
a perfect time of day
and weeding in my garden I
contentedly will stay.

Alas how sad it is that this
serenity won't last,
and tranquil summer ev'nings will
a thing be of the past.

For up on the horizon
a cloud waits on the wing,
and when the time is right, this cloud
disrupt will everything.

A plague of midges will descend
one night out of the blue,
what devastation it will wreak,
what chaos will ensue.

On man and beast alike those fiends
alight for blood to drill.
upon their hosts their jaws will lock
till they have drunk their fill.

With fiendish glee they settle down
to make a meal and soon
their wretched victims driven mad
for mercy importune.

Disciples of the Devil they
well earn his accolade,
and legion are the plans of man
to which they have put paid.

There is no antidote, no cure,
for man the outlook's bleak,
the midge ad infinitum will
on him its havoc wreak:


## NOBODY'S CHILD

The Ancient Romans landed here
two thousand years ago,
and inadvertently they seeds
did of destruction sow.

They brought the rabbit with them and
since then it's multiplied
and though its foes are legion
the rabbit has survived.

Their young engaging are. There must
be few they fail to charm,
and yet there are those, who will these
defenceless creatures harm.

The rabbit is a herbivore,
its staple diet grass,
its appetite for all things green
its downfall is alas.

This being vegetarian's
a serious defect,
for many is the turnip field
a rabbit fam'ly's wrecked.

The rabbit to the farmer is
a most destructive pest,
and with plotting its extinction
the farmer is obsessed.

They vengeance on the rabbit take
with gun and snare and gas,
and with myxomatosis did
infect them all en masse.

To carnivores upon the ground
the rabbit is good fare,
and buzzards, hawks and eagles
prey on him from the air.

The frequency with which they breed
ensures they will survive.
It matters not how many die
there's plenty left alive.

For that I'm glad though he's a pest
his only fault is greed,
the world would be a sadder place
without his gentle breed.

## BESIDE THE SEA.

It's pleasant any time of year
to be beside the sea,
But spec'ly in the summer time
because there's lots to see.

The beach no longer empty is,
but dotted here and there
with fam'lies on their holidays
enjoying the sea air.

The caravans and tents, it seems
have sprung up overnight,
they're parked and pitched upon the grass
within the camping site.

The children with their spades and pails
build castles in the sand,
and there are adults happy to
give them a helping hand.

In little knots go beachcombers
on a collecting spree,
heads bent, examining the beach
for treasures from the sea.

A few have braved the cold to swim,
into the sea they stride
and surfers too, in their wet suits
upon the breakers ride.

The ones that cannot swim down at
the water's edge will be,
they may not swim but still they like
to paddle in the sea.

Among the dunes in marram grass,
high up above the shore,
there winds a trail that beckons
the intrepid to explore.

The dogs with life are well content,
their luck they can't believe,
the walks they go, the swims they have,
the sticks that they retrieve.

The men and boys delighted are
to kick a ball about,
displaying soccer skills that would
delight a talent scout.

On windy days, quite mesmerised,
looking up at the sky,
are those who like to watch the kites
cavort about on high.

With all the social evils that
we read of ev'ry day
It's somehow reassuring to
see families at play.


## FOR WHOM THE HEATHER WEEPS

I'm getting on, I doubt I've not
got very long to go.
My eyes are dim, my joints are stiff,
my reflexes are slow.

Life has been good, I'm well-content
to have survived thus far.
I've come through many barragings
and not a single scar.

I do not have the bounce I had,
with old age has come fear.
Another year has gone and now
August 12th looms near.

This year I think will be my last
with being not so fit,
my mind I don't think's sharp enough
the shooters to outwit.

They'll come with beaters, dogs and guns,
over the moors will spread,

The ground will have a carpet of
my kinfolk lying dead.

Exploding guns and barking dogs
will tear our nerves to shreds,
and yet if we want to survive
we'll have to keep our heads.

Life is precarious. Both fowl
and beast upon us prey
but they take only what they need
their hunger to allay.

Not so with man, sadly there is
no limit to his greed.
To conservation we have found
he doesn't pay much heed.

Ironic, is it not, that they
the 12th call glorious?
Can slaughter then be noble or
carnage illustrious?

If Death is stalking this Red Grouse
and this 12th is my last,
Lord let the bullet strike my heart
and make my going fast.

# IN MEMORIAM

As Summer's manic pace abates
and she goes down a gear,
Autumn is waiting in the wings
and soon she will appear.

The Summer's passing Nature marks
a flower does select,
with which she wreathes the hillsides in
a token of respect.

The Heather fam'ly she has picked,
the Ericas and Ling,
they flower in a colour fit
for emperor or king.

The hills and moors, majestic are
in shades of purple cloaked.
They, in the setting sun at night,
in golden light are soaked.

The bees upon the flow'rs descend,
their humming fills the air.
To make their honey, they the flow'rs
of pollen will strip bare.

Red Deer among the heather roam,
the stags with antlers crowned.
They rulers are, their kingdoms wild
on windswept hillsides found.

From curlews, winging overhead,
does sad, sweet music spill,
a wild lament that climbs and swoops,
throbbing o'er moor and hill.

## SEPTEMBER

September is a pleasant month,
a respite for a while.
The fierce glare of the summer sun
replaced by Autumn's smile.

The garden birds return to base
free now of fam'ly ties,
out from the robin pours his song
as round his patch he flies.

The flocks of geese will soon be here,
you'll hear them as they fly,
if you look up, you'll see the V
that they make in the sky.

In garden, wood and wayside place
the trees with fruit abound,
and in the hedgerows, hip and haws
and brambles can be found.

Chantarelles, fly agaric, the
keps and such like fungi,
in wayside, wood and field you'll find
of them a good supply.

The creatures of the wild enjoy
a banquet unsurpassed,
they must stock up to overcome
cold winter's icy blast.

September is a pleasant month,
it's neither hot nor cold,
a gentle, kindly interlude
'ere winter gets a hold.

## OCTOBER TAPESTRY

If I were asked to say which month
held special charm to me,
I think that out of all the months,
October it would be.
It takes me back down through the years
to days that were carefree,
to childhood days of innocence
set out for me to see.
I have a picture in my mind,
a bright and vivid one,
a tapestry of memories
with Autumn colours spun.
Hues yellow, russet, gold and brown,
my picture has them all,
and captured on the canvas
is the glory of the Fall.

I see a carpet, made of leaves,
spread out upon the ground.
The hawthorn, rowan and wild rose
with berries red are crowned.
The spiders' webs, sprinkled with dew
are sparkling in the light.
Up in the sky, a harvest moon
shines down on us at night.

I taste the first potatoes in
their jackets, caked with ground,
and the ripe fruits from the garden
with which the trees abound.
The walnuts and the hazelnuts,
the fruits of Hallowe'en,
and the apples that we dooked for
all shiny red and clean.

I smell the ripeness of fresh fruit,
plum and pear and apple,
the oiliness of all the nuts
especially Brazil,
the fusty dankness of the woods
with fungi harvest rich.
The smoke of bonfires burning leaves,
tattie shaws and rubbish.

I hear the song we chanted as
around the fires we danced,
the high-pitched laughter of a child
with Hallowe'en entranced,

The crunching of the nut shells
when the nutcracker squeezed tight,
the honking of the wild geese when
we chanced upon a flight.

I feel the thorns of brambles that
are tearing at my skin,
the damp earth on potatoes that
we've helped to gather in.
The smoothness of the conkers that
have never seen a fight,
and the tacky soldiers' buttons
that to your clothes stuck tight.

If I were asked my fav'rite month
October it would be.
With all its happy memories
it is the month for me.

# AUTUMN

Though Summer's nice I must confess
I'm glad to see it wane,
I like the rhythm and the pace
of Autumn's sweet refrain.
Set as it is 'tween two extremes
in gentler mould it's cast,
gone is the fierce heat of the sun
to come cold winter's blast.

The countryside is yellow-gold
with fields of waving grain,
the farmers rush to harvest it
before it comes on rain.
From dawn till dusk the clatter of
the combines fills the air,
they'll carry on until the fields
of grain have been stripped bare,

In wood and hedgerow, verge and field,
the wild fruits are displayed.
On ev'ry tree and bush the clumps
of berries are arrayed.
In gardens and in orchards are
fruit trees in Autumn gown,
with apples, damson, pear and plum
their branches are weighed down.

The birds' frenetic pace has eased,
their young have left the nest,

To the reaping of the harvest
their thoughts are now addressed.
The animals are stocking up
for hard times lie ahead,
the abundance of the harvest
ensures they are well fed.

A little elfin Van Gogh has
been painting in the night,
with gold and yellow, brown and red
he's set the trees alight.
His expertise with colour bright
is on the leaves best seen,
at some point he ran out of paint,
he left some evergreen.


## THE HARVEST

The combine's cut and threshed the grain
and left a stubble field,
the trailers to the barn have gone
with this year's precious yield.
The oats and barley straw is stacked
safely in the steading.
There is plenty grain to eat and
straw to make the bedding.

It's a battle with the weather
to get the harvest in,
and there is much rejoicing
if we the battle win.

The hay was cut and baled and built
in stacks around the field,
or baled and wrapped for silage in
black bags which were well sealed.
The loads of hay the tractor towed
were for the hayshed bound,
the silage bags were neatly laid
in rows upon the ground.

It's a battle with the weather
to get the harvest in,
and there is much rejoicing
if we the battle win.

Of Golden Wonders and Kerr's Pinks
there has been a good crop,
they're lying in the shed in heaps
with scattered straw on top.
Considering it's been so dry
the swedes have done well too.
The yield is good enough for us
to see the winter through.

It's a battle with the weather
to get the harvest in,
and there is much rejoicing
if we the battle win.

# THE LITTLE MOTHER

I'm really very angry with
my little Bantam hen,
I'm sure she has a clutch of eggs
in the walled-in garden.
I haven't found them yet because
they are too well hidden,
if only she'd content herself,
scratching in the midden.
I've told her it's the wrong time to
indulge in motherhood,
October's far too cold a month
to raise a little brood.
I'll need to find her hiding place,
if not I'll be too late,
and some little cheeping chickens
will meet me at the gate.
I'll wait until she comes for food,
I think that would be best,
then I'll sneak up and follow her,
returning to her nest.
I'm sorry Mrs. Bantam you
can try again next year,
but don't wait until October
your family to rear.

# **OCTOBER**

October is a month that must
appeal to one and all,
we've surely all remarked upon
the glory of the Fall.

The leaves have made a carpet
and laid it on the ground,
red, yellow, russet, gold and brown
in all their shades are found.

In garden, wood and wayside place,
in hedgerow and in field,
the richness of the harvest is
on bush and tree revealed.

The oat and barley crops are in,
the stubble fields are bare,
the smell of burning tattie shaws
is hanging in the air.

The feathered winter visitors
with native residents
will banquet well on Mother Earth's
Autumn beneficence.

On the last night of October
the guisers can be seen
with lanterns and a bag in which
to put their Hallowe'en.

October is a month in which
there's something for us all,
so long may it enchant us,
long may it us enthral.


## JOLLY GOOD SHOW

The sun was shining,
it was warm, a pleasant autumn day.
The noise and bustle of the town
seemed very far away.

The peace was shattered by the sound
of rifles going off,
a shooting party had arrived,
the whim of some rich toff.

This time it was the pheasant they
were out to execute,
with rifles and with dogs they would
it hound and persecute.

All afternoon, so it went on,
report after report.
No doubt the wholesale slaughter would
be looked on as good sport.

The pheasant runs along the ground
till panicked into flight,

emitting as it takes to wing
a raucous screech of fright.

It can rise quickly off the ground
and get to a fair height.
But it is then incapable
of a long distance flight.

Some pheasants are quite tame for they
with barley have been fed,
the keepers fill their feeders so
the toffs can shoot them dead.

If pheasant shooting is good sport,
then someone tell me why,
what skill is there in shooting it,
if it can hardly fly?


## THE LAST LAUGH

The pheasant isn't blessed poor thing
with much intelligence,
sometimes however it displays
a modicum of sense.

Sometimes the birds fly on to an
adjoining neighbour's land,
the 'sportsmen' have to let them go
for shooting there is banned.

## OUR ROBIN

I see we have a robin back,
he hasn't been here long.
He's marking out his boundaries
and claiming them in song.
On roof, on shed or rowan tree
perched singing he will be,
he's telling all the neighbourhood
this patch belongs to me.

He sits upon a wire between
our chimney and a shed;
to get a better view below
he cocks his little head.
One beady eye is fastened on
what's happening down below,
he's wondering if the lady to
the bird table will go.
She comes out ev'ry morning with
some fat, some crumbs and seed.
He's always first to see her and
the first to have a feed.

Last year we had a robin too,
perhaps it's the same chap.
I kept a watch on him and tried
to save him from mishap.
He showed off most outrageously
his aerobatic skill,
till one day he zoomed near enough
for Puss to make a kill.

I prised the cat's jaws open,
thinking my robin's dead.
Imagine my surprise when he
flew up over my head.

I'm glad our little robin has
decided he will stay
for he will help to brighten up
a cold, dark, winter day.
If I put out some food for him
I know he'll sing for me,
in his little bright red waistcoat,
perched in the rowan tree.


## HALLOWE'EN

On the last night of October
strange things are to be seen
but that is quite acceptable
for it is Hallowe'en.

All the children have been busy,
themselves they have disguised,
they've taken great care to ensure
they won't be recognised.
They call on all their neighbours and
perform in fancy dress,
what child it is performing,
the neighbours have to guess.

With bags for nuts and apples and
a lantern to give light,
on all the houses roundabout
they plan to call that night.

There are apples in a basin,
with water it's been filled.
Underneath there are some papers
in case the water's spilled.
A child is crouching, watching
the apples down below,
if only they would stay at peace
then she would have a go.
At last they settle and her head
into the water tips,
what screams of pleasure can be heard
if she an apple grips.

False faces, masks and witches
and children in disguise,
tangerines and apples, nuts
in ev'ry shape and size.
On the last night of October
strange things are to be seen,
but that's to be expected
for it is Hallowe'en.

# GUY FAWKES

On the fifth day of November
sixteen hundred and three
crowds were gathering in the streets
King James the first to see.

The State Opening of Parliament
he would attend that day,
but first the premises were checked
the King's fears to allay.

The soldiers, in the basement found
evidence of a plot.
Gunpowder, stowed in barrels to
the basement had been brought.

Guy Fawkes, the man behind the plot,
that very day was caught,
and he and his associates
were soon to trial brought.

Of treason and conspiring
'Gainst King and Government'
the plotters were found guilty
and to their deaths were sent.

The fifth day of November is
when we commemorate
Guy Fawkes and his compatriots
plotting against the State.

Bonfires are lit,
on top there is an effigy of Guy,
and rockets, sparklers, cath'rine wheels
explode into the sky.

On the fifth day of November
gunpowder, treason, plot,
assassination anarchy
had Guy Fawkes not been caught


## LEST WE FORGET

The War (they said) to end all wars
for four long years it waged.
An Armageddon on the fields
of France and Belgium waged.
In summer time the poppies grew,
battalions of them spread
across the fields and meadows in
a vivid splash of red.

And when at last the guns were quiet,
the earth was stained dark red,
beneath the scarred and barren waste
in millions lay the dead.
And many were the young men that
of life had been bereaved,
and many were the families
who for a loved one grieved.

The poppies grow again each year,
a wreathe for all the dead,
and tossed by gentle winds they are
a waving sea of red.
Nature again her harvest reaps,
a part of some great plan,
her healing touch repairing all
the damage done by man.

Lest we forget the fallen in
the carnage and mayhem,
a day is set aside each year
when we remember them.
The poppies, growing in the fields
where so much blood was shed
a symbol are, by wearing one
we honour all the dead.


## THE WREN'S PRAYER

It says in Your Good Book, O Lord
that should one sparrow fall
You know it and are vexed because
You care about them all.
That being so I wonder if
Good Father could You then,
if You have any time to spare,
protect and guard the wren?

Because we're small, we quickly chill,
our bodies lose their heat.
In freezing temp'ratures we die
without enough to eat.
May we all find a cosy place
cold winter to survive,
let there be seeds and insects too
to help us stay alive.

May all male wrens find plenty leaves
and grass to make a nest,
with lots of little baby wrens
may parent birds be blessed.
To feed our young, please let there be
of food a good supply,
good Father with some help from You
the wren will multiply.

Guard and watch over us O Lord,
from predators us shield.
When danger lurks may we find holes
in which to be concealed.
Dear Father please accept our thanks
for anything You do,
from rock and wall, in song we shall,
repay our debt to You.

## HOPE

It's very cold, it's dismal,
it's a bleak December day.
And heavy clouds block out the sun.
snow can't be far away.

But there's a little breath of Spring,
here in my living room,
a bowl of hyacinth has quite
dispelled the winter gloom.

Tiny white bells, in cluster cling,
like grapes on ev'ry bloom.
Their fragrance on the air is borne.
it permeates the room.

From little shoots I've watched them grow
to what they are to-day,
what beauty, what perfection in
their innocent display.

Mother Nature is not dead,
she is alive and well,
These bulbs upon my windowsill
have broken Winter's spell.

# DECEMBER DELIGHTED

I remember when I was young
on dark December nights,
drawing the curtains in the room
and switching off the lights.
The room was warm and cosy for
the fire was always lit,
and right in front of it upon
the floor I liked to sit.

I liked to peer into the fire
to see what I could see,
the glowing embers pictures made
that fascinated me.
Sometimes a blue flame would appear,
a harbinger of snow,
and on the chimney, oval shapes
of burning soot would glow.
Heaped on the fire were logs and coal
so that it would burn well
and if the logs were wet they had
a salty, kipper smell.
They'd hiss and spit but to the heat
at last they would succumb
and little bubbles of their sap
up out of them would come.

My gaze would travel upwards. There
were other things to see,
for on the ceiling and the wall

the shadow flames would be.
The shadows flared and flitted in
the flickering firelight
and I would sit entranced and watch
a dark December night.


## WINTER WONDERS

Once we get older winter is
the season that we dread.
When morning comes, it's dark and cold
we'd rather stay in bed.
With stiff old bones and creaking joints
our way we slowly make
and gingerly on ice our steps
with trepidation take.

Poor Winter cannot hide her faults,
they're plain for all to see,
She's ruthless, unpredictable
and wayward as can be.
But this capricious maiden can
bewitching charms display,
and with her sparkling beauty she
will take your breath away.

A silver moon is shining down
upon the earth below,
the stars are twinkling in the sky,

they sparkle and they glow.
Hard frost has made a carpet
of crystals on the ground
and on the branches of the trees,
it tinsel strands has wound.

The glory of the sun, when from
night's prison it breaks free,
a red sun disappearing as
it sets over the sea.
Smoke curling from a chimney pot
dispersing up on high,
the silhouettes of winter trees
against a winter sky.

Yes, winter's unpredictable,
often misunderstood,
but she, we'll see just as she is
whatever be her mood.
With wind and sleet and ice and snow,
her downside we well know,
but so too we appreciate
her charms when they're on show.

# THE DONKEY'S CAROL

The little donkey gratefully
began to eat his hay,
with Mary on his back he had
come many miles that day.
A humble beast of burden, used
to ridicule and scorn,
yet he a chosen witness would
that night see God's Son born.

Now patiently he'd borne his load,
followed where Joseph led.
In Bethlehem the inns were full
but one innkeeper said,
"I'm full up but you're welcome to
sleep in my cattle shed.
At least it's warm and you will have
a roof over your head."

The cattle shed was warm and dry,
it smelled of fresh, green hay,
and on the floor, upon a bed
of clean straw Mary lay.
The little donkey lodgings shared
with cattle and some sheep,
warm and well fed he settled down
and soon he fell asleep.

When startled by a sound he woke
sometime during the night,

Glancing across the cattle shed
he saw a wondrous sight.
Beside Mary and Joseph was
a manger filled with hay
and on the top in swaddling clothes
a new-born baby lay.

Some shepherds on a hillside heard
a choir of angels sing,
they hurried to the cattle shed
to see the new-born King.
Much later too came wise men,
they had journeyed from afar,
with gifts for the new King, they had
been guided by a star.

In years to come the donkey would
ponder upon that night,
how he, a humble donkey had
witnessed a wondrous sight.
And when he was abused by man
and felt sad and forlorn,
it warmed his heart remembering
the night the King was born.

# COMPASSION

The night was bitter cold,
hoar frost had carpeted the ground
and on the branches of the trees
had strands of silver wound.

Along the track came travellers in
the disappearing light,
a fam'ly searching for a place
in which to spend the night.

Bowed down with weariness they trudged,
feet dragging on the ground,
from Bethlehem they'd come that day.
for Egypt they were bound.

As Joseph scanned the hills he saw
a little way ahead,
a hill-path, veering off the track.
up to a cave it led.

Holding the baby, Mary climbed
cautiously up the slope,
and right behind her Joseph dragged
the donkey on a rope.

Tired out with their exertions for
the hill path had been steep,
as soon as they had eaten they
would need to get some sleep.

A spider watched with in'trest from
a web within the cave
and when she saw the little Babe
her heart a lurch it gave.

Poor mite, she thought, what can I do
this bitter cold to stave?
I know, I'll spin a web across
the entrance of the cave.

My web of gossamer should help
to keep the cold at bay.
The little Babe if he is warm
should sleep the night away.

She set to work immediately,
in no time she was done.
Across the entrance to the cave
a silken wed she'd spun.

A troop of soldiers later on
came swarming up the path,
Their orders were to find the One
who'd incurred Herod's wrath.

They reached the entrance to the cave,
before they entered in,
their captain stopped them. "Look," he said
"There's no need to go in."

"That spider's web in front of us
means we need not delay.

It's in one piece. It would have torn
had someone come this way."

And so the soldiers carried on,
their footsteps died away,
the family could sleep in peace,
no harm would come their way.

The moon was bright and down upon
the cave its light did shed.
Touched by the frost, the spider's web
looked spun with silver thread.

So we, each year at Christmas time
our tree with tinsel drape,
rememb'ring how a spider helped
the holy child escape.

# **THE LITTLE BEGGAR-BOY**

The streets were thronged with people and
traders their wares did ply
and in a lane there stood a man
watching the world go by.

In that same lane outside an inn
a little begger sat.
His cheeks were pinched. His body thin
crouched on a thread bare mat.

Man: Poor little waif, why are you sad?
      It's been a busy day
      Your bowl is full. You should be glad
      for you'll eat well to-day.

Boy: Yes, I'll eat well. I'm glad of that
      but where am I to bed?
      The sheets are full. For me that's bad
      where will I lay my head?

Man: Fret not but go to yonder inn.
      You'll find a cattle shed.
      Some have already settled in.
      They'll let you share their bed.

Boy: That's where I'll go the cattle shed.
      Perhaps they'll let me share.
      There in the straw I'll make my bed,
      sleep in a stable bare.

Man: Look at the star up in the sky
    as you go to your bed.
    Take care a new-born Babe's asleep
    within the cattle shed.

Boy: I'll see no star, no little cot.
    I'm blind since I was born.
    I won't see with the eyes I've got
    a little Babe new-born.


That night as Bartimaeus slept.
He dreamed and he could see.
It was so real he thought this can't
be happening to me.
His dream was of a Babe new-born
who was a King of Love.
Of peace on earth angels did sing.
A star shone up above.
Some shepherds came. They'd seen the star.
They knelt beside His cot.
Later came wise men bearing gifts
to give the One they sought.
When Bartimaeus went next day
into the busy street
the stranger from the day before
again he chanced to meet.

Man: Well young fellow, how are you
    last night how did you fare?
    These people that I spoke about
    did you their lodgings share?

Boy: It happened as you said it would.
      Now I a debt must pay.
      I am beholden for my dream,
      My dream of yesterday.

Man: Your debt you can repay if you
      Work for the Prince of Peace
      One day there will be peace on earth.
      One day all strife will cease.

Boy: That I will do, I'll work for Him
      A way I'm sure to find.
      Throughout my life I'll strive to be
      a lover of mankind.